RAY MEARS

vanishing world

RAY MEARS

vanishing world

a life of bushcraft

HODDER &
STOUGHTON

To the elders who so generously shared their wisdom and experience with me and who remind us all what it means to be part of the human family.

introduction

My father was a printer who appreciated the way photography recorded history. He gave me a complicated manual 35mm camera when I was a child, even though I was far too young to fully appreciate it – or know how to use it. But his enthusiasm got me started.

Many years later, when I started writing about the outdoors for a magazine, they would send a photographer out to take pictures of the things I wanted to cover. When I looked at the photographs I was always disappointed, so I thought 'Why don't I take them myself?' That's how my love of photography began.

I found that I enjoyed photography as much as writing, so I decided to try taking pictures for other magazines. I joined an organisation that sent out newsletters advising you how to become a professional photographer. One of their bits of advice was very good and very simple: browse a newsagent's shelves for a magazine whose photographs you like and feel that you could take, contact the editor and ask if you can show him your portfolio.

Twenty years ago there was a new magazine called *World*, a beautiful, glossy British version of *National Geographic*. I phoned the editor, an Italian gentleman called Mark Ausenda, and said, 'Can I come and see you with my portfolio?' Much to my surprise, he said yes. I put the phone down and thought, 'Oh my goodness, I need a portfolio!'

I already knew the kind of transparencies that *World* magazine wanted so I put my best images together in a slide sheet and off I went. Mark came down to the foyer of his office building and I handed him my slide sheets.

This is Mark Ausenda, who was the editor of World *magazine. He also had a passion for mushrooms. Sometimes we would leave London at four in the morning, head out to areas that I knew were good for mushrooming and fill our baskets before the start of the day.*

He held them up to the light and said, 'Yes, thank you, they're not good enough'. I was incensed. At first I didn't think he'd actually looked at them closely enough, but of course he had. I asked him what was wrong with them. Mark sat down and took time to explain that they weren't sharp enough and the definition wasn't right. So I said, 'OK, I'll be back'. He gave me a look that suggested he thought he'd never see me again.

I decided to sell my existing camera, a shutter priority Canon with a cheap telephoto zoom lens, and bought my first serious camera, a Nikon FM2 with a 35–105mm lens. For six months I taught myself to take better pictures and then went back to see *World* magazine. Mark met me in the foyer again, looked at the new pictures and said, 'They're still not good enough... but come back again'.

That was a strange position to be in, and I wasn't sure what to do next. I decided to give myself an assignment, as if he'd commissioned me for the magazine. I wanted a subject I already knew about so I set to and made some of my own stone tools – a bone needle and some sinew thread and so on – then I got every copy of *National Geographic* I could find. I searched for any pictures of similar subjects to give me an idea how they photographed them.

I had no idea how they achieved the results, but I did notice several things: the pictures were very sharp, they had strong colour in the background and they were artistically lit.

I got some coloured paper, two rolls of the best Kodachrome 25 film, a sheet of glass and some bricks. I put the stone tools on the glass and I hired an extra flashgun, because I could only afford to own one myself.

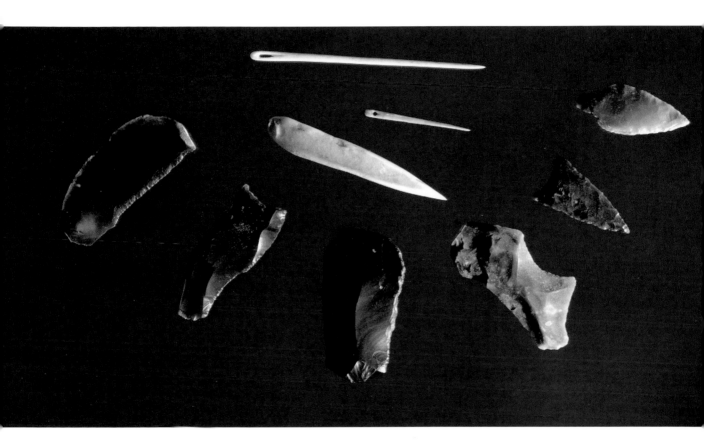

These images of stone tools (here and overleaf) brought me my first photo assignment for World *magazine.*

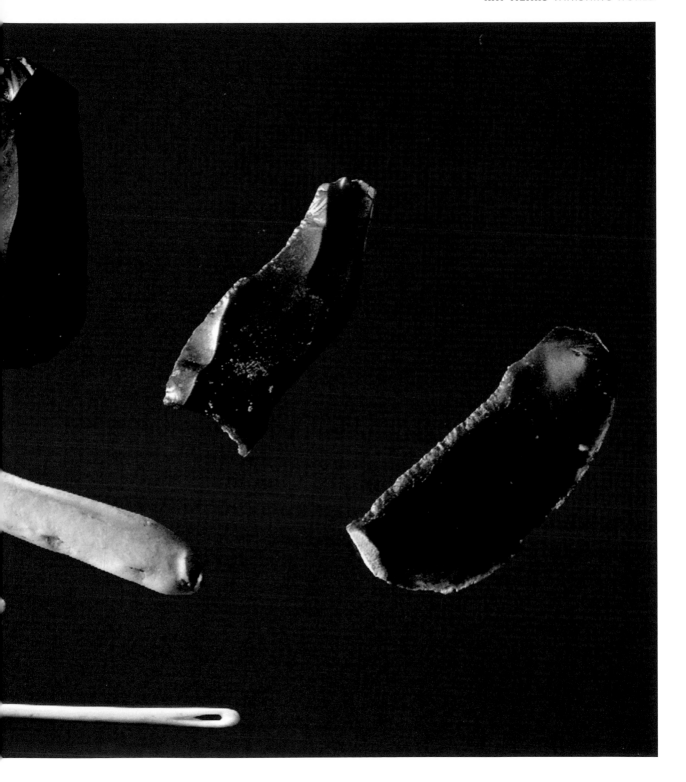

Dr Chris Stringer, researcher at London's Natural History Museum, with a wax cast of an early hominid skull. World *magazine encouraged me to take quirky images, but they only used half of this one, which I shot all in one frame.*

Now I could use one to backlight the stone tools and one as a front-light, so that not only would the individual facets show but they would also be slightly translucent with the different colours behind them. I took pictures with a number of different coloured backgrounds, put them on the slide sheet and went to see Mark again.

This time he took a look at them and said, 'Yeah, come with me'. We went into his office, where he put them on his light box then called his assistant editor in and asked her what she thought. She said, 'Wow, the colour, the sharpness'. And I walked out with my first assignment.

A week later I was taking photographs of some of Britain's most precious fossils behind the scenes at the British Museum, and really without a clue what I was doing. That's how it started. I learned a lot about photography by working for that magazine and I was sent on all sorts of strange assignments – covering donkey abuse in Ireland, swords, kites – all very challenging. Every week or so I went into the *World* office and they would give me a big crate of Kodachrome and off I went in search of results.

The hardest thing about photography is getting to the image. Taking photos is the easy bit. Getting yourself into the place where the image is, seeing it – that's the hard bit.

World were very demanding as a magazine. They wanted images with maximum depth of field, absolute clarity, sharpness *and* creativity – which, when you're taking photographs on location in Britain in winter, is really difficult. It forced me to school myself in all the different techniques of photography.

This image was used for an article on eighteenth-century smuggling. It was quite a tall order to photograph eighteenth-century scenes in the twentieth-century but I had great fun photographing these re-enactors, who enjoyed living the part.

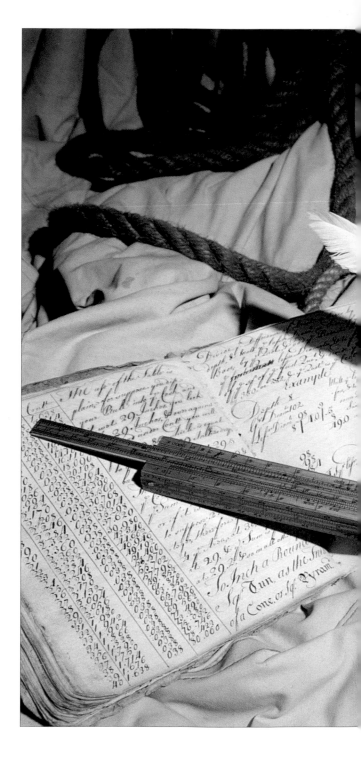

My picture of smuggling equipment. It wouldn't have worked without the rope and canvas. It shows various tools used by Customs and Excise in the eighteenth-century to measure the specific gravity of alcohol and find hidden compartments on ships.

More images that were used for an article on eighteenth-century smuggling.

Photography can be broken down into different genres: landscape, still life, reportage, and so forth. For *World* magazine I needed to have an understanding of all of these disciplines. One early assignment was to take photographs to go with an article on smuggling in eighteenth-century Britain. I got in touch with Customs and Excise and found they had a collection of old smuggling equipment. I imagined that their office on the bank of the River Thames would be an old building with a window where I could lay out the smuggling stuff in some really lovely natural light. Their guy said, 'Yeah, yeah, we've got windows, it should be fine'. Something about his tone made me think that it might not be exactly as I hoped, so I threw an old rope and some canvas into the back of the car with my camera equipment. I got there to find it was a completely modern office block with fluorescent lighting. Fortunately I had the canvas and the rope so I could create a still life setting and make it really moody and I got the shots. That was a good lesson learned – be prepared.

Those are the kind of little tricks that you learn when you work for a magazine. You've got to come back with the money shot. And you can't wait seven months. Sometimes I look at *National Geographic* and think how lucky their photographers are to have between six months and a year to do an assignment, sometimes shooting hundreds of rolls of film. I was trying to get three good shots from every roll of film, and I'd only have a morning to take them. That was really good training. It taught me to handle a camera, to handle it quickly and to handle it well. But I made some terrible mistakes along the way.

One day I was covering an article on wartime secret agents. I had all these people who had been wireless receivers for agents' messages coming from Europe gathered together, and I was going to take two group shots on the steps of a wonderfully grand building. They were really difficult to organise into groups. They just wanted to chat and this picture session was an inconvenience for them. Eventually I got them all lined up and shot a whole roll – without any film in my camera. I was so hassled that I hadn't noticed.

Time pencils, detonators and a Sten gun used by the Special Operations Executive (SOE) during clandestine operations in World War Two.

Veteran SOE operators posing with suitcase radios that were used to transmit messages from behind the lines in occupied territory. The radios still work. I was incredibly impressed by how understated some of these highly decorated men are.

A miniature spy camera used by SOE. I lit the picture to convey a sense of moonlight and the atmosphere behind the lines.

Ironically *World* magazine closed down a short time later, which was a great shame.

Photography is like life: you make a lot of mistakes to begin with but unless you've made those mistakes and lived with the consequences you don't really know how to achieve success. I think you go through different phases as a photographer, almost as if you go through different moods.

I like landscape photography but people are what really interests me. How you relate to the subjects who are represented in your images is really important. You have to build a trust with the camera. That can be tricky, especially if you're photographing people who have been badly photographed, or who have never seen a photographer before and are not sure what you are doing. It's a real challenge, and it's zen-like.

This is a picture I took while on an assignment for World magazine in the South of Ireland. He has to be one of the last generation to travel in this way. This was a normal sight at the time but it is vanishing fast.

You try to get into a flow where you are not really thinking about the technique.

There's a recent picture of a group of three young Australian aboriginals (see page 196), where one of the things that makes that photograph a success is my eye line. I knelt down to take it and that brings a certain dignity to the photograph, which echoes what I felt about those people. When I take pictures of pygmies, they don't look small. There's no sense of scale because I don't like that. To me they're giants in their world, and that's the most important thing – to see them as they might see themselves.

In a digital world I still prefer the magic of celluloid. One of the reasons I don't like digital photography is because of what is called 'chimping'. You take a photograph and then you look at the screen on the back of the camera to see whether the image worked or not. I hate that because it immediately breaks the connection you have with your subject. If you're working in a more old-fashioned way, you take one picture and you take another. Each time you are sketching with the camera, and eventually something comes from that but you're not sure what your pictures are like until they're developed. If you keep reviewing all the time, you're breaking that connection and it becomes just a technical process.

You can see that in photography today. Although digital photography is improving all the time in terms of the clarity of the image and the resolution, I don't see many images with a digital origin that inspire or excite me. When you see images by Cartier-Bresson, for example, decades after they were taken, you realise how much has changed and even disappeared in photography.

One of my most important images is a photograph I took of some pygmies (see page 188). When after some difficulty I was able to convey my respect for them, they burst into song and started clapping. To me that was the first time in my photographic career that I had captured a 'moment'. Capturing an instant is the essence of photography. That's why I think photography is an art because you are responding to light, to form, to shape, to composition. What makes photography different is that the way you capture your image is literally a slice of reality: a symbiosis of external events and the photographer's emotion. It's a moment absolute.

Capturing that precise moment, when all the elements are there so that your emotional connection with the subject is captured on celluloid, is very difficult. It's akin to hunting, to releasing the trigger on a rifle. It has to be exactly the right moment, and there's a strange feeling when it happens. You know when you've got it sometimes because it feels almost like fate. It's a very profound feeling. In a lifetime as a photographer you may only take five or six images that you'll be happy with − or maybe even only one. Other people may like a lot of what you take but I think inside yourself you're always seeking something more from the next image.

I find it fascinating, and I love photography. I go through periods when I don't take photographs at all but I always see images. If I'm not happy then I can't take pictures. I have to enjoy what I am doing, which is interesting. When I look back over the photos I've taken at film shoots, there have been times when it's not been going well because of personality clashes or time constraints and there can be other times when I've taken film

*A gypsy camp in Country Cork.
I was surprised how traditional life
still was in the South of Ireland in the
late 1980s.*

Portaging is hard work but it's just a normal part of canoeing. The angle of the tree suggests this will be an uphill journey. Everyone who has ever carried a canoe over a trail will smile at this picture.

after film after film because it was just such a great experience. Today I struggle to capture emotions photographically even in adversity.

By its very nature photography documents a world of vanishing moments. In the following pages is a collection of such ephemera: people, places and events collected from some of the journeys I have made over the past twenty years while documenting and recording tribal and first nation cultural traditions and bushcraft. I have selected images that convey a sense of being there, quiet moments rather than loud.

When I began this work I didn't realise that in many cases I would be witness to the last generation of elders who had actually lived a wholly traditional lifestyle. At work even their movements and posture were meaningful, embued with the subtlety and nuance born of experiences lived throughout a lifetime. As these elders have passed to the next life so their experiences and an incredibly rich knowledge of nature – in many cases the very foundation upon which their cultural identity is built – are lost forever.

Ray Mears, Sussex 2008

Capturing a moment from a shoot in Canada. Today I very often use a Leica Rangefinder. With an SLR camera, when you press the shutter you lose contact with the subject momentarily as the mirror lifts, but this doesn't happen with the Leica Rangefinder, making it easier to capture the moment.

Jacob is demonstrating a traditional Inuit means of obtaining water. He's made a small fire from bits of wood cut from one of the cross members of a sledge. Underneath the fire is some seal blubber, burning on a piece of sealskin. Above it he's propped a chunk of freshwater ice from the iceberg on which he is standing. As it melts the water is dripping down underneath the sealskin at the bottom of the fire and then running through a channel cut to allow it to fall into a cascade of small depressions. The gulleys between these are filled with soft powdery snow, which filters out the tars and the oils that the fire taints the water with, until at the bottom you get fresh drinking water.

It was a very special moment; I'd never seen this technique before or even read about it anywhere. And as I presented a piece to camera explaining how it worked, behind the camera all the old men were giving me the thumbs-up, saying 'Yes, that's how it really is'. And they all had memories of having to do this. This is another of the old skills that is passing with the arrival of the coleman stove and the zippo lighter.

The little V you can see in the distance in this photo is the town of Pond Inlet on the headland at the top of Baffin Island, and we're standing on top of an iceberg in the frozen inlet.

A Kalahari Bushman burying an ostrich eggshell filled with water. This is the way they would store fresh water in the bush, enabling them to hunt and travel over longer distances. Today this technique has all but vanished with the arrival of the plastic bottle, or often an old oil can pressed into service as a canteen – which is much easier to find and stronger than the eggshell.

The real secret here isn't knowing how to blow the ostrich egg; the real secret is knowing which grass to use as the bung. Not just any grass can be used; the right type swells to provide an airtight seal preventing evaporation. It's those kind of details that are lost first, and with them the very function and practicality of a technique.

To me this picture symbolises everything about being human in this environment. An Inuit artist has taken the ice itself and turned it to a work of art. It shows the confidence that the Inuit hold about their life in such an unusual and challenging environment. It means: 'We can live here'.

The Abenaki or Waban-Aki inhabit the forests of southern Quebec and northern New Hampshire. Message trees, like this one, were normally to be found at the point where a small stream joins a river. The bones and skulls of animals that had been hunted in the territory are hung on this tree, both as a sign of respect to the animal, whose spirit will return to the forest, and also as a guide to show others what has been hunted in the area, providing an instant means by which a hunter can assess how much food has been taken from that land and act accordingly for conservation.

Other features are found on the tree. Sometimes dried berries are left there, both as offerings and also for use in an emergency. In times of war, blankets and other supplies were buried at the foot of such trees. On the side of the tree is a small wooden cup carved from a burl. If it was placed face in, as this one is, it meant that the nearby water was not safe to drink; with the opening facing outwards it meant the opposite.

This is an important photograph to me, taken while I was working with the pygmies in the Central African Republic. This girl is getting a drink from a water vine under which she has just washed herself a few minutes before. These beautiful, gentle people of the forest live deep within my heart.

While I was there I was shown a box of matches that had been given to a group of pygmies by a Westerner who'd been living with them. They went off into the forest for two years then they returned and gave him back the box of matches and not a single match had been used. That is part of the magic and the dignity of these people; they are not dependent on outside aid, but of course this is one of the things that is vanishing.

As long as the forest remains there is the potential for the pygmy to remain and as long as the pygmy remains, the knowledge of the forest remains. Without them biologists would strive for generations to acquire the same knowledge.

Maybe when this Mongolian girl grows up she will remember the time when she got milk directly from the sheep rather than from a bottle in a supermarket. Who knows? That's the kind of change that is happening all over the world; and everyday moments like this are precious in the passing of different lives. Each evening the sheep are tethered head to tail for milking. There is a remarkable degree of trust between these people and their animals.

These men are making rope from horse hair. Three men standing out of shot have rotated pieces of wood attached to each of three strands. The strands are held taut and passed through the latticework wall. On the inside they are twisted together into a rope. It's an age-old Mongolian tradition that will vanish the moment cheap polypropylene rope becomes available – because why go to all the hard work when you can buy an alternative cheaply? And yet the knowledge is the most important thing.

Traditional Siberian boots made by Evenk reindeer herders, shown alongside the materials, parts and tools used in their manufacture. Starting from the left, there is a knife made out in the forest then two tools used to scrape and soften hides. Next there is a shin skin, which is a very strong part of the reindeer, hence its use for footwear. It has been tanned and then scraped and softened. Below that are back sinews of reindeer, which make the threads that are used to sew the boots together. The many different components are required to get a good fit. Inside the boots, dry sedge of the genus *Carex* is used to make a sock, after it has been dried and beaten to make it soft. For very cold conditions inner boots are made with the fur inwards – and very warm they are too.

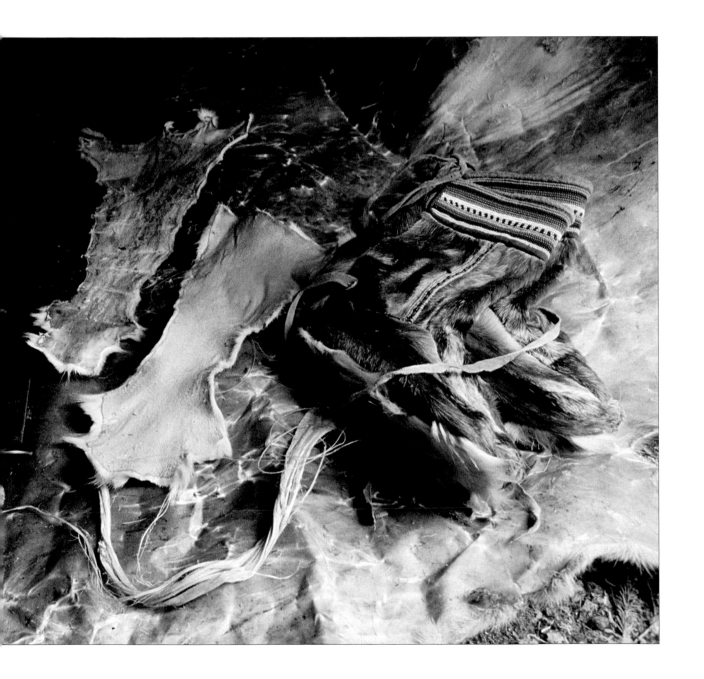

When making the roof of a house with palm fronds, this Sanema man has to place them very carefully on the rafters and compress them with great dexterity to ensure that it will hold out during Venezuela's tropical storms. The roofing leaves must be cut in the correct moon phase to ensure that they are not full of moisture, which would cause them to rot. They make up a thick overlapping layer, which will last for several years and will provide an incredible habitat for insect life.

The Sanema are incredible weavers; this picture shows a beautiful basket being made featuring an intricate pattern of spider monkeys. The craftsmanship they display is quite astonishing and is usually inspired by traditional folk stories. In the rainforest there is a superabundance of suitable weaving materials, particularly the splints from palm fronds seen here.

Here at Minganui in the centre of New Zealand's North Island, some Maori people are heating rocks for a *hangi*, an underground oven that will be used to roast a meal for the whole community. A young child is helping to prepare the fire, learning how it is done. This image of a continuing culture appeals to me more than the dramatic moments when the oven is opened.

Wilhelmina, an old Montagnais woman we worked with in northern Quebec, is scooping out the brains from a caribou's head. These will be used to tan the caribou's skin. Her hands show the experience of a lifetime working in this way.

She's a very traditional Innu woman. Time spent with people with this experience over so many years is priceless. In the background there is a fox skin hanging up and a pair of *mukluk*s similar to the ones she will be producing.

I've long been fascinated by commonplace events. When you're visiting different cultures it's all too easy to get drawn in to the dramatic and dynamic forgetting the commonplace, but this image shows a scene of traditional Inuit life, the kind of thing that happened all the time. Ham is softening seal blubber for use in the traditional lantern, the *koodlik*. He's using a hammer made from caribou antler, which they call *tuktu*. I was keen to capture that sense of being just round the corner − although you don't find many corners in a world where the surfaces are round, as with an igloo.

To ensure true whites I used an old-fashioned selenium handheld meter, which is not dependent on batteries and is therefore more reliable in extreme cold. Snow is a fascinating material and challenging photographically as the colour changes in different shades from brilliant white to the deepest blue according to the light and time of day. Here I wanted to capture the brilliant whiteness of late morning in the Arctic. It's the fact that it's just a small moment in the day that really attracts me to this photograph.

This is the *koodlik* in situ; it's the traditional means of cooking and heating inside an igloo. In the old days they were carved out of soapstone but today they're hammered out of sheets of metal when they're used at all. This old Inuit tool is being replaced by the coleman petrol stove, for which they require fuel to be shipped in.

The *koodlik* uses traditional local materials; you can see softened seal blubber liquefying at the edge of the flame. The wick is made from *shaputi*, a mixture of the seed heads from dwarf willows and dried moss.

Eventually the flame will burn the whole length of the *koodlik*, if carefully tended. The house-proud Inuit wife will ensure that the flame burns evenly, with no flares. Not only does a *koodlik* smell better than a petrol stove, but it's also a beautiful lantern and it's absolutely silent. Silence is what this photo is all about – a silence that was a fundamental part of traditional Inuit life and is being destroyed by the roaring petrol stove.

The Hadza inhabit the baobab forests that border Lake Eyasi in Tanzania. I have very fond memories of two trips I made there to spend time with them. Here they are making fire by using a uniquely long stick as a hand-drill. All the men carry a bundle of arrows with their bow and in amongst these arrows will be their fire-stick. They select the hearth wood straight from the bushes when they need to make fire. This is the most enduring method of primitive fire-lighting worldwide, and probably the most common. To me it symbolises bushcraft in its purest sense.

Since this picture was taken the Hadza are being moved off their traditional hunting grounds, which are being set aside as a private hunting reserve for wealthy hunters. What a shame; these people would make the most amazing wildlife rangers. It's typical, though. Hunter-gatherers are in many ways on the bottom rung of life's class structure and they suffer accordingly.

Kalahari Bushmen making fire using a hand-drill. Their sticks are somewhat shorter than those of the Hadza and they normally work as a pair. In the background a director takes a picture as we witness a skill that is gradually vanishing. The sticks they're using are from the manketti tree, which is a producer of both food and fire-sticks. It's a haunting image – a scene from their life that hasn't changed for hundreds of years but will shortly be gone.

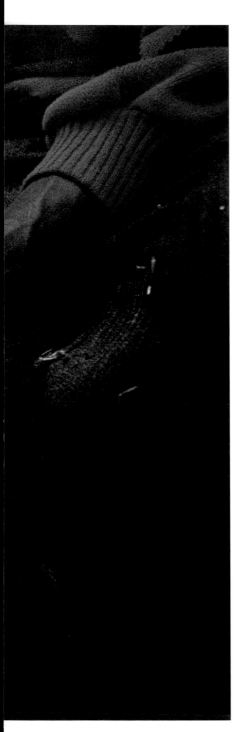

One of the rarest methods of making fire is the fire plough. While travelling in the Central African Republic I heard people talking about this technique, which they called *kombo-kombo* (also the name of the wood that is used). Eventually I managed to find a village on the banks of the Zaire River downstream from Kisangani where people still remember this method and we went into the forest to watch a demonstration. The young men knew how to make fire by this method but no longer had the energy to succeed; it took an old man to come along, shoo the young men away and say, 'No, this is how it's done.'

The fire plough is not an easy way of making fire. It has great symbolic significance and there are sexual connotations – which is true of all fire-sticks. The stick that is brought to the hearth is the male part and the female is the hearth and from the union of the two a new life is created. A new fire, I think, which is still sacred today – as anybody who has ever learnt to make fire by this method will attest.

I have great respect for this man; he really had lived the old life here in Arnhemland and was my first aboriginal tutor. He's trying to make fire with a hand drill but he is very old and is struggling. He got close to making the ember glow and would run out of energy. The young men offered to help him but he wouldn't let them as they didn't know how. When I offered to help he said: 'Yeah, that's fine'. He was telling the young men that they should have taken the time to learn this technique from him while he still had the energy to teach them.

Every boy in Western Samoa is expected to be able to make fire very quickly using a fire plough. The hearth and the plough wood are all made from coastal hibiscus; for tinder they use the husk of a coconut, which you can see just to the right of the plough.

This man was very amusing to work with. While we were filming, if we asked him to repeat something he seemed to think we were trying to catch him out and make him slow down; he would obligingly get faster and faster for each take, which made for difficulties in continuity. Eventually he was asked to demonstrate the manufacture of a shelter and he launched into the rainforest with a machete and had completed his task before the camera had even started recording.

This picture will immediately be identified by those who know the northern forests of Scandinavia, but will mean nothing to anyone else. To most it is just a fire, but those who have travelled with a Sami in northern Scandinavia will recognise a typical Sami fire, where the burning logs are raised on stones to provide a good through–flow of air. If extremely cold green birch is burned together with spruce it gives a slow, hot fire.

Some 200 or so kilometres inside the Arctic Circle, the Taiga is a beautiful environment that I've come to know extremely well. It's sunset, and when I look at this picture I feel deep inside that I need to light a fire for warmth for the coming night. Standing under the Arctic sky is unique. You feel as though every molecule of warmth is being blotted out of you by the almost malevolent cold.

I look at the forest and I think of all the secrets that it holds: the lynx, the reindeer, the Siberian jay. It's a wonderful environment but a place

where you can't make mistakes. You have to follow Nature's rules implicitly and that way you can observe the wolverine rather than have someone come across the scraps and remains of your body after you've been scavenged by it.

For many this is a threatening environment, but it's a place I've learned to call home. That's one of the joys that bushcraft brings. This photo shows a simple scene; but in some ways it is the simple scenes that move me most because of the potential they evoke.

The Namib Desert, just inland from the Skeleton Coast, is an astonishing place. There are dunes and rocky desert and here, in this picture, you can see the remnants of hunter-gatherers' homes: little stone circles that were once huts, now standing proud on the surface. Archaeology rises to the surface in deserts as the sand is blown away, literally exposing the past and giving the impression that the previous inhabitants vacated the location just yesterday. It's a mysterious site and incredibly evocative, in one of the harshest landscapes on earth. Places like this fill the mind with questions. Who lived here? When? Where did they go? Where are their descendants now? It's an oasis of mystery in a world of endless information.

I was struck by the bleakness of this location, deep in the Namib Desert, and the way the sand dunes march across the rocky ground. If we could watch with time–lapse photography you would see them striding across the landscape; they're the real masters of this environment. In some native cultures people believe that the rocks have life. And in places like this you come to think that way.

In the foreground is a dollar bush, which relies on the tiny sand dune that shelters behind it from the wind. The sand holds moisture that the bush needs. As the dune grows bigger so can the bush, and as the bush grows so does the dune. I love the interconnectivity of the two.

This photograph shows the Plough, or the Big Dipper, with the Northern Lights passing through it. It's one of the great joys of spending a lot of time outdoors that every night you see the stars in the sky and occasionally you get real magic like this.

This beautiful, timeless landscape shows the mist gathering in an inlet in British Columbia with glaciers in the background, millpond-calm water and the forest spreading upwards. It's moments like this that make my heart sing and I just want to capture these emotions with the camera when I encounter them – but it's not always easy.

This picture was taken on a winter's day in Norway, when the skies were still quite dark. It's daytime and yet the Northern Lights are illuminating the clouds.

It's said that rocks are alive and I believe that's true. The nature of rocks is to suffer silently, to remain calm and unmoved by the worst of weather and in places like this when the weather is testing, you only need to look at the environment around you for inspiration about how to cope. To live embued with the stoicism of a mountain rock, able to endure and withstand adversity, is something all people who inhabit wild places must learn. This photograph shows Norway's Hardangervidda plateau in February.

Orion has been my friend on many, many journeys. It's the hunter in the sky that watches over us and it would be wrong to do a book of pictures of the outdoors and outdoor places without including Orion.

My film crew have just arrived on a small airstrip near an Indian village in Venezuela and the locals have come out to meet us. Things have really changed; the first time I arrived in a village like this I was surrounded by people who wore few clothes, had feathers in their hair and were adorned with paint. Just eight years later we are in the same part of the world and we are surrounded by very modern people, and I realise there is great change occurring here. Such changes are inevitable and bring many benefits for the people but at significant cost: the social upheaval can have a devastating impact upon the families, and new food production methods are rarely as well adapted to local conditions as the more traditional methods.

When you arrive in communities like this you have to make sure that you have had health screening so you don't bring any illnesses with you. It's so remote they haven't had the exposure to illness the rest of us have experienced.

The fern forests of central North Island, NZ, have got to be seen to be believed. There is a quality here I really like. I love forests. Forests call to me in a very strange way. And in this forest there are ferns occupying places that otherwise would be spaces in all the other forests that I know. Even in the rainforest it's not quite like here. There's a very special feeling in this forest.

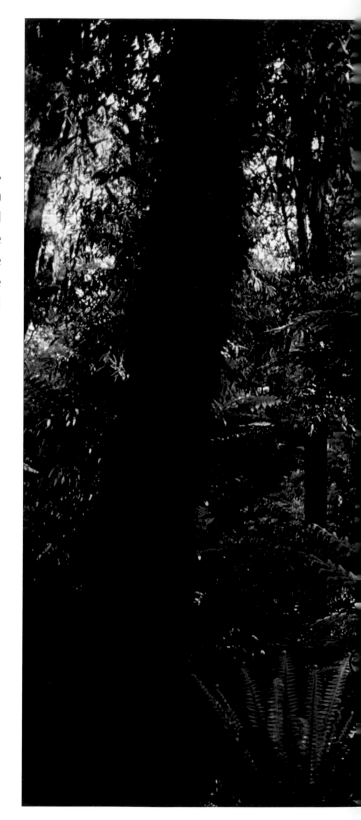

Barry Foster and Sam Cox, my film crew, wearing caribou clothing as they work with the Inuit. You can lie down and fall asleep at –35ºC in this sort of clothing. It's an incredibly difficult place for a film crew to work, particularly in February; just keeping the equipment functioning requires immense skill and diligence, and it takes special people to be able to do this kind of work. There's a traditional sledge behind: that's how we transported some of our equipment.

Ham is just beginning to build an igloo, laying the all-important first ring that sets the angle and the slope, which will culminate in the final block going in at the apex.

Two elders from Pond Inlet, Baffin Island, who built an igloo for our filming. It was very important to find old men to work with on this occasion, men who had lived the life instead of just having learned the skill, and both of these two grew up in igloos as children. Ham Kadloo on the left vividly remembers going on a hunting trip with older men when he was a small boy. And their skill in igloo-building is remarkable. Although igloos are still built, the subtlety of having lived in them is being lost, so it was a real privilege to be able to spend time with these gentlemen on the ice.

They're wearing two different types of footwear: Ham, on the left, has boots with polar bear fur on the soles for cold, dry conditions; and Jacob is about to go seal hunting so he's got his wet weather boots on with the black sealskin outers.

Their caribou-skin clothing is traditional, lovingly made by the women of the community, who knead and pummel it until it's incredibly soft. The functionality of these beautifully fitted garments can't be emulated by modern clothing.

An igloo at sunset, and behind it is a source of fresh drinking water – an iceberg. This image evokes memories for me of the wind: the sound of the wind, and what a silent world it is. Traditionally, of course, the igloo would have been filled with the sounds of the family – children laughing and playing games with one of the many different types of traditional toy – as well as the smells of the food being cooked. Today igloos are largely built for tourists, or for educational purposes, but they lack that buzz of family.

And so here, on my first trip to the very far North, was a sense that things were changing, that the world was losing cultures and skills. It's remarkable to realise how these people lived, using the most abundant material around them – the snow – in such an efficient and pragmatic way.

One of the things that human cultures round the world have in common is the sense of a hearth. In Britain we think of a pub on a rainy night with a warm wood fire burning to welcome passing travellers; and you get exactly that same sense here with the igloo illuminated solely by the light from a *koodlik* giving this dark orange glow. Whenever possible I try to capture the reality of a location. All too often people will use photographic lights to over-illuminate the insides of these places but I like to try and capture things as they actually are.

As the night falls, the cold seems to envelop you in this landscape and just having this little cupola of snow warmed by the tiniest of flames ensures life. And all of a sudden the skill of tending the flame of the *koodlik* gains greater importance and we realise that it is a survival skill in its own right. Because without that tiny flame the warmth from the shelter is lost and that can make the difference between maintaining or not maintaining the vital 37ºC that we require as a species to survive.

This Skeleton Coast shoreline was once walked by hunter-gatherers, known as the *strand loepers*, or I guess you could call them beachcombers. They would make shelters from whale bones that washed up on the coast and carried spears made from oryx antlers. I reconstructed this shelter for a television programme using sealskins from a local tannery. It gives a sense of what these strange shelters would have been like; they have peculiar echoes of a culture more Stone Age than modern.

These Masai are at an *olpul*, a place away from the village where the young men are taken and taught the skills they will need for life. On the fire they are cooking a medicinal soup made with goat's blood and an infusion of the bark of the native pear – *dombeya* – and this will make them strong and fortify the youth.

The cultural identity of the Masai is passed on in their *olpul* so the cultural tradition survives strongly amongst them. The young men learn how to take care of themselves in the bush; where to find soap; how to make fire; how to behave when they encounter an elephant or a lion. They learn stories of the past; ultimately they learn how to be Masai. And because of places like this, their cultural sense is, I think, more well-established than for many other tribal groups.

This shows a shelter built during a woodlore course in northern Lapland. It's an open lean-to with a long log fire reflecting in warmth and heat, and it symbolises for me how important fire is. Fire is the tool that human beings use to modify the environment around them and it is the thing that makes us human. Other creatures use tools but none use fire in the way we do. Here it dispels the cold of the Arctic night and brings its timeless cheer.

Susan and David Swappie are Naskapi people we filmed with in Northern Quebec, and here they are building their *whiskechanchuap* traditional shelter. The name means 'Whiskey–Jack's Nest' and Whiskey–Jack is derived from *wiskechan*, the Indian word for the Siberian jay. This bird always has its young in the forest in winter and is always found close to a campsite. Their presence is a cheery thing, although the hunters of old didn't like them because the bird could sometimes give away the presence of a hunter.

The Nuaulu live on the island of Seram in Indonesia – part of the Spice Islands – and there are five clans within the particular group that we worked with. We built this shelter in the forest, and they made a feast of a mixture of bat and wild pig, which has been cooked in bamboo tubes for the occasion. After taking the photo I joined in. Despite what an outsider might think, the meal was delicious and the atmosphere one of great enjoyment with much chatter and laughter – a very fond memory.

***Ger* is the Mongolian name for a yurt.** Here a mother is making tea in the traditional way. The interiors of all the yurts I saw were well-ordered and beautiful, almost like a stage set. Nothing is random. Every part of the *ger* has a purpose. It is the woman's place and she is in charge.

You get a sense from this photo of the geometry of these incredible mobile shelters. The walls are made of a lattice of willow laths tied together at their intersections with rawhide. These walls fold flat concertina-style for transportation. The roof is made up of beams that radiate out from a central boss. Over this framework a thick, insulating felt covering is stretched, then made weatherproof by the outer canvas covering. Traditionally *gers* were transported by camel but more often today they are moved by lorry. Although portable, they provide an incredible feeling of permanence.

The Evenk of central Siberia live in tepee structures they call *chums* and this is a typical interior scene with a tin, wood-burning stove with a chimney in the centre. Hanging from the lodge poles are reindeer shin skins spread with small sticks they are drying.

The old man on the left is called Arkardi. He's sitting on a bed made of spruce boughs, while in the distance Yuri is threading a needle with sinew for sewing. It's another one of those moments that, no matter what your culture, we all share. The difficulty of threading a needle after the age of forty when your eyesight is deteriorating is something that links us all.

The Evenk don't just use *chums* as teepees; they also use ridgepole tents, which are another classic feature of the northern forest. The three axes in the logs outside tell you that there are three men in the tent, because nobody goes into the forest here without an axe in their hand.

This photo was taken in September and the temperature was –8ºC.

There is no land in this photograph; this is the frozen world that the Inuit know. They would traditionally travel huge distances in a nomadic style across the frozen ice, finding a living in the most astonishing ways. Large communities would have trouble finding sufficient food to stay together for any length of time, so they remained in small groups.

Mobility was very important. Here you have the traditional Inuit husky team on traces made from sealskin. Sealskin is incredibly strong and it won't freeze or become brittle in cold weather. It's strange that these dogs have never seen a tree but if you stand still for more than a couple of minutes they know exactly what dogs do to trees – and you have to be careful not to end up with wet feet.

When I look at this picture I can recall with great vividness the sound of the dogs: their eagerness and boisterousness when getting ready to take off in the sledge. And the incredible freedom and independence that the sled symbolises in the vast Arctic landscape.

Nothing is more important in a leopard's life than hunting. As time goes by I watch predators with increasing fascination. I can relate to the way our ancestors revered them. Their knowledge of leopard behaviour, the muscle structure, the inner workings even, are evident in the way they are depicted in rock art all over the world. There's something very captivating about watching a leopard. Here their patterning shows up clearly against the sand but as soon as they move into undergrowth, if you take your eye off them for a moment, they vanish.

This is one of my favourite wildlife photographs. It shows a young vervet monkey suckling and in a strange way it serves to remind us how closely we are related to these creatures. I often wonder what they must think when they watch tourists passing by in safari parks: 'What are those strange monkeys up to now in another one of those strange white vehicles?' Who knows?

When I'm travelling I like to be silent in the woods, invisible and yet present, able to witness the normal everyday lives of the animals. It's the more intimate moments that I find very special.

Giraffes are incredible creatures, moving very gracefully without seeming to move at all yet covering huge distances. In the background there are some acacia trees. These have evolved to suit the climate close to the Equator and animals have also played a part – their grazing causes the development of thorns and other defence strategies – showing just how connected everything is with everything else around it.

We watched a cheetah stalk and, after great effort, bring down the Thomson's gazelle – and within a few minutes down came the vultures. They cruise at very high altitude and have the most incredible eyesight; the moment they spot something on the ground that is of interest they descend, swooping down. And, of course, no sooner have they started to glide in to the kill than they attract other scavengers to the site. A few minutes after this photograph was taken a young hyena came and picked up the gazelle and ran off with it in its mouth as though it was a bone.

A lot of people don't like vultures; they look at them and say they're ugly and they symbolise something dark, but in fact they are a very important part of the eco-system – cleaners-up – and there is a beauty in them. Perhaps what is sinister is the thought that they might clean up after we have gone ourselves. But there is a beauty in watching nature go about its activities in a natural and cohesive way.

Here amongst the shattered rock of this incredibly bleak landscape on the Skeleton Coast, the black–backed jackal finds a perfect opportunity to utilise its camouflage. They approach very close, thinking they won't be disturbed or spotted – but of course they are.

Grizzly bears are much maligned. They have a fierce reputation that they don't really deserve. Yes, they are a strong animal and in certain circumstances they stand up and proclaim their dominance over an environment to which a human is but a visitor. But they are also a beautiful animal and there are tender moments to be observed. Here, on the Pacific coast of British Columbia, just before the arrival of the salmon, bears can be found on the shoreline looking for mussels and seafood or eating the sedge grass, which they are partial to. A few minutes later this mother swam across the estuary with her cub on her back. They're very good swimmers.

They are an incredibly intelligent animal and I've never had a bad experience with one. I like them and I enjoy the encounters – and it's nice to know that you're not the top of the food chain when you visit an environment that they are lords of.

This lone male is looking for females who are coming into season and that's the most important thing on his mind – which is fortunate because he ended up just a metre away from me. If he encounters a male cub he will likely kill it because that is their way. But he still needs to put on some weight for the coming winter. He's got a bit of feeding to do. This is in the Kutzemateen Reserve British Columbia, a national park especially for the grizzly bear. They don't like humans encroaching on their territory so it's important that land has been set aside where they can find the solitude they require. To go to such a place is in many ways a spiritual pilgrimage and I have very fond memories of spending time here with grizzly bears.

This juvenile bald eagle swooping through the landscape of British Columbia is a wonderful creature. Later it settled on the shoreline and I was able to approach in a canoe and very quietly drift up to the bird. It knows no waterborne predator so I managed to get within a few feet of it to sit and watch for an hour. Spending time in wild places with wild creatures in close proximity is really what bushcraft is all about. Sometimes that is forgotten when we become blinded by techniques; but the techniques of bushcraft are just the stepping stones to adventure.

These strange specialised ants, which live deep underground, store a form of sugar in their swollen abdomens. The women of the Central Australian Desert follow the tiny holes and excavate their way underground until they come to hidden chambers where these ants hang from the ceiling, then they collect and eat them. They taste just like barley sugar, and are an important food. It reminds me how in depth the knowledge of aboriginal people is and how necessary such knowledge was to survival.

This has got to be the strangest mode of transport I've ever seen.
Mongolian people are quite remarkable in the way they tame and work with animals such as camels and horses, who they even milk. They live in an incredibly harsh landscape of vast open grassland where the wind always blows.

We had finished a long day's filming in Mongolia and the crew were in their yurt recharging batteries and cleaning lenses when I took a stroll and encountered these camels. The light in this land is just astonishing – in any direction, at almost any time of the day, on almost any day of the year you will find magic. For me the exposure to such a treeless landscape bordered on agoraphobia but was more than compensated for by the warmth of welcome that I received.

The Evenk tame reindeer and use them both to carry their equipment and to ride. The reindeer here are slightly larger than those found in other parts of the boreal forest and they can travel very quickly through the landscape.

The dogs in the Evenk camp where we stayed almost went unnoticed because they're so well–behaved. The Evenk don't put up with dogs that misbehave. The tip of this one's tail was missing where it had suffered frostbite. These beautiful animals are a constant, ever–watchful part of Evenk life.

The Evenk catch reindeer by setting up an improvised trough made from a tree and filled with salt. The reindeer come to lick the salt and then the Evenk are able to lasso them. Some they will slaughter for food or other important goods; the rest they may tame and use as pack animals.

I don't just take pictures when I'm overseas; I'm equally as interested by the things I encounter here at home. Grass snakes are absolutely beautiful. This one had a scar on his back so I named him Scar. I found him one day trying to swallow a toad but it had puffed itself up and there was no way he was going to manage. The toad released a poison from the glands behind its eyes, forcing Scar to let it go and his anger and disgust were clearly apparent. All the time we live our lives, other animals are living theirs alongside us and it can be a cat and mouse existence in the predator/prey relationship.

This is deep inland on Baffin Island. A hole has been cut through eight feet of ice – which takes quite an effort – and the hunter is jigging a little narwhal ivory lure in it to attract Arctic char. He has a leister spear ready to impale any inquisitive fish when they come into range.

This was a very traditional means of obtaining food for the Inuit. Their knowledge of their environment is astonishing. Knowing where to place the hole was a big part of the story. Elders would leave rocks on the edges of the lakes to indicate the places that were good for netting or spearing fish. As knowledge is being lost from these cultures, and as the more remote and isolated fishing-holes fall into disuse, those rocks now sit silent and wind-blown.

Although I took this picture in February, the hunter is wearing his summer parka because the locals gave us their traditional clothing so that we would be warm enough. He is wearing traditional trousers and special boots, with black moccasin outers on the bottom, made from sealskin and tanned in such a way as to be waterproof: the traditional footwear for fishing.

These Kalahari Bushmen are hunting with tiny bows that shoot poisonous arrows. The arrows have no fletchings and their accuracy is questionable at long range, but that's not how they're used. The idea is to get close to the animal and get the arrow to hit it anywhere because then the poison does the work. I've had the great privilege to be able to travel with old men who are still experts in this technique.

Since the arrival of bore holes in Bushmen communities the people have become settled and are no longer nomadic. The result of this is that the traditional knowledge of the environment is passing. The nuance, the detail, the experience of having lived the life and walked the trail is disappearing. And that does make a difference.

Here the men are hunting off to one side and they've shot a volley of arrows towards their target. I've witnessed this many times; when they shoot an animal they will check to see if they were successful and then leave it and come back in a couple of hours. When they get back, they pick up the animal's trail and collect it wherever the poison has finally caused it to give up the ghost. In Africa there are many different arrow poisons used by different cultures; but wherever you go people know about the Bushmen and the strength of their poisons.

These remarkable boats are built in the same way as rafts, yet in them the fishermen of southern India brave one of the strongest tidal swells in the world to get out to their fishing grounds and put their nets down in search of prawns. Each morning half of humanity seems to awaken on this beach. As far as the eye can see there are people. The boats are carried down into the waves and then there's an incredible journey as they fight their way through the surf to get out to their fishing grounds. No easy harbour here.

Most of the Bushmen I've worked with have a wonderful easy manner. I find them to be honest and upright individuals with a very good sense of humour and lots of energy, particularly when it comes to their traditional skills. They are so at home in the bush, it's a real privilege to spend time with them and it makes you realise that no matter how long you were to spend there you could never emulate them. These Bushmen are smiling, because they're never happier than when they're hunting.

Bushmen use these long poles for catching spring hares, which are like a cross between a hare and a kangaroo that burrows underground. The poles are used to hold the animal in its underground lair until it's dug out. The Bushmen paused to enjoy the rainbow in the distance just as we did – and you feel a kinship at times like that. We are from very different worlds, we wear very different clothes, we look physically different, we speak a different tongue, and yet intrinsically at heart we are one people.

An old aboriginal man in Arnhemland is demonstrating how to catch fish using a spear with a woomera – which is a stick with a notch that fits at the end of the spear and acts as an extension of the arm, providing greater accuracy and swiftness to the throw. If it was windy he would blow water out of his mouth to gauge the direction in which the wind might deflect the spear.

This is a Sanema man in Venezuela, painted with traditional war paint and holding arrows and a bow; and at the tip of the arrows are bamboo points covered in a poison that is made from the virola vine. When we filmed here in 1996, life was completely traditional. In the background you see the tube basket used to extract cyanide from grated manioc roots.

Visiting places like this is like going to another planet — or was at that time. Of course, this traditional way of life is greatly threatened, as is all traditional life within the South American rainforest.

Traditionally the Nuaulu were renowned for head-hunting but I found them to be remarkably adept experts in the rainforest. This man, with a pig-hunting spear and his parang, is completely at ease in the forest. And he's smiling rather than looking threatening. I have respect for the Nuaulu people, and that is reflected in the photograph, as is the relationship I developed with this individual.

These pictures were taken in 1996, the first time I worked with the Kalahari Bushmen in a small village close to the Botswana border. In the picture opposite, one of the Bushmen elders is about to enter a trance during the trance dance. The images on the following pages show people of all ages sitting around the fire singing as the dance takes place. It's a wonderful, very primeval sound that takes you right back to our roots when you hear it. Bushmen have an incredible sense of rhythm and harmony and they don't all clap in tune or clap in time but the overall effect is very pleasing. It reaches deep within and stirs some hidden part inside us, some latent memory of a time gone by.

I often sit by my own campfire at night here in the UK and look up at the sky and think about my friends in Africa who are sitting by fires there, dancing and singing. This is one of the images that has stayed with me. In subsequent visits to the Kalahari I have witnessed other trance dances but somehow, as time has gone on and people there have become more used to interference and visits from outside, the hidden secrets of the Bushmen are held more closely to their chests.

This rock in the Central Australian Desert is of great significance to aboriginal people. I was very privileged to be taken into the desert and down a Dreaming track by an old aboriginal woman. This is one of the sites of her Dreaming and she entrusted me with knowledge of this place, which I cannot share because of a bond, a promise given. However, she told me a story associated with the rock that can be passed on. When I walked around the base I found small chippings of quartz and she said: 'I remember the day those were made. That was my grandfather – he was making a point to go on the end of a *miru*'. That's a kind of spear thrower used in the desert. She said when she was a little girl she used to climb up on top of these rocks and her mother would shout to her: 'Come down, come down, if you fall you will hurt yourself'. And so when I look at that rock I remember her and I remember the story as she told it and I wonder about all the other rocks that I've walked past whose stories have been lost.

This is a Montagnais man – a Shaman – we met in Labrador. We were working with an old woman who remembers this man from her youth. We filmed him singing and playing the drum and telling us about the role of the Shaman, who would go into a trance to find the caribou. Once he located them he would hold them where they were with a special song, which had charms to stop them moving on before the hunters reached them.

While we were filming, Wilhemina, the old woman, came and sat beside me and smiled and nodded and she was very happy to see the traditional things being practised again. I asked her: 'Which is better – the new or the old world?'

And she said: 'The old world was better.' Despite all the modern advances and the modern houses that the people live in she felt the past was better, because there were fewer problems with alcohol and other substance abuse, and there was less debt and the people were happier – even if they worked harder.

This Shaman of the Nuaulu is praying to his ancestors to bring him luck with a pig trap he's just set in the forest. He's making an offering of beetlenut. These traditions are so easily lost and yet so interesting. Very often they disappear in the face of more aggressively marketed religions and yet at their core they imbue a sense of respect in our relationship with the forest. I think that in their loss we lose something of ourselves and our dignity as a species on this planet. We manipulate and control such a lot of the natural world but these traditions remind us to be more respectful to the features over which we seem to have dominion.

This Bushman soothsayer is using a small, beaded piece of skin to interpret what the spirits want him to do. We visited him before we started filming and he is asking the spirits' advice about the fee he should negotiate. The spirits didn't negotiate a particularly good fee so we re-interpreted their request, but we found it amusing nonetheless. The Bushmen can take this kind of thing very seriously but at other times it can just provide humorous entertainment, depending on the circumstances. It is easy to forget that hunter-gatherers have a sense of humour just as we do. It often comes out at just such moments.

This old aboriginal man from the Walpiri people is depicting a spirit ancestor for whom he holds Dreaming. It would be wrong to mention his name or the name of the ancestor that he depicts, but what happens is that the man carries with him the sacred teaching of the dance and the song and at times like this he will vanish into the bush. The next time you see him he will be adorned as the spirit ancestor. At that point, to all intents and purposes he has become the spirit ancestor embodied and will act, perform, speak and do as the ancestor would. Soon after he has made his appearance and his statement he will vanish back into the bush and a short time later he will re–emerge from a different direction dressed in his normal clothes and unaware of what has gone on. I believe it's very important to show great respect for these traditions; not to analyse or judge them but just to accept them.

One of the most memorable projects I've ever been involved with was telling the story of the remarkable efforts made by the Allies to destroy the Nazi attempts to create an atomic bomb. In one of the narrowest valleys in the world at Vermork, near Rjukan in Norway, the Germans had taken over a factory producing heavy water. A group of saboteurs – Norwegians who had fled from Norway after its occupation and been trained in the Scottish Highlands – were parachuted into the mountains to destroy the factory. I think in their heart of hearts the men believed they were going to their deaths. Instead of laying two-minute fuses in the factory, they decided to use thirty-second ones. They knew the mission was important, although they didn't know until much later exactly what it was they were destroying.

After the factory exploded, the gods smiled on them and they were able to make a swift escape and climb to this incredibly remote mountain plateau, known as the Hardangervidda. The gentlemen photographed here are the survivors of that attack. They are standing at the top of the cable car that leads from the valley bottom to the hilltop. All of them told me that when they climbed here that morning they looked out and saw a mackerel sky that was clearing and they knew they were safe. It became a sacred place for them. This was the last occasion on which Klaus Helberg climbed the mountain and looked out over his favourite peak before he passed away. And it was a very special moment. Not much was said but a lot was felt. It was a privilege to be there on this occasion – sixty years almost to the day after their mission.

Jake Korell (seen here with his dog Keese) is an amazing, quite eccentric man who has spent his whole life trapping in Wyoming. He was thrown out of school for using bad language and because he smelled too strongly of the skunk he spent his time trapping. He lived for most of his childhood in bunkhouses on ranches with men who could remember the last days of the Wild West, and in many ways Jake embodies that spirit. There's a peace that comes from knowledge of the land and Jake possesses that, despite his feisty nature. I asked him how it was to grow old and he said: 'I never pal around with people my own age; they slow me down.'

I went into a forest in the very southern tip of the Central African Republic to spend a couple of days with the Mybaka pygmies and try to learn about their life. Pygmies hold a very special place in my heart. My interest in bushcraft was in no small way encouraged by a wonderful book called *The Forest People,* written by Colin Turnbull, that described a year he spent living with the Ba Mbuti pygmies of the Eastern Congo. These are a different group, further southwest, but what a remarkable experience it was!

There were several things that struck me: the upright posture of the pygmies; the great pride they have and their confidence in their knowledge of the forest. The forest is their home and they seem to be indivisible from it − almost part of it, like a leaf. I had a local Bantu guide to whom I would speak French and he would translate for me. But Bantu think they are superior to pygmies so when I said, 'These people are fantastic − they're professors of their forest', he was unwilling to translate it. I insisted and eventually he did reluctantly translate what I had said. This picture shows the moment the words reached them and they burst into song. They were happy because of what I'd said and from that point on as we went through the forest they sang the praise songs that they have for the plants and trees around them. And it brought a new dimension to their existence in the forest.

For me it's a very important photograph. I think it's the first time that I captured a 'moment'. It taught me a lot about working with indigenous cultures and has inspired many similar experiences since. Sadly, the forest where these pygmies live is shrinking and ironically they are often employed to fell the very trees upon which they depend.

This Hadza man is chewing the remains of a small antelope, which they'd shot a few minutes before and cooked immediately on the fire. He's chewing the ribs to get the marrow out. We couldn't pronounce his name so we nicknamed him Ringpull because of his unique head-dress. Why does he use ringpulls for his head-dress? Why not, if it makes him happy?

A Hadza man who is studying herbalism, Mustafa is a very upright man and a future elder of the community. He has an astonishing knowledge of nature; all hunter-gatherers have a good knowledge of nature but even amongst them there are those who specialise and he is just such a person. In men like him are the hope for the future.

This charming aboriginal woman showed me how to make grass seed damper (an unleavened bread). The softness of her manner shows the warmth these people possess. They have been victims of racism for generations yet I have only had good experiences with aboriginal people. They are receptacles of astonishing biological knowledge and it's a pity that the modern world hasn't found a way of recognising this. Maybe some sort of educational qualification could be established as a measure we could use in our world.

We had all worked really well together, they had just danced the magpie dance, we were happy, respect buzzed in the air, the sky was strangely cloudy and cool, and there was a natural atmosphere. I had tried several shots of the dancers before it all came together in this image, which resonates with trust, confidence and hope. In the political world outside of Arnhemland, all was negative press for aboriginal people – but here in the bush we knew the truth.

I've worked with Barrie Foster, a cameraman, for over fifteen years now. Here we are in Labrador at -40ºC, but this is a man who thrives in the cold. He's a fantastic companion to work with. No matter how difficult the going is, he never loses the ability not just to function but also to remain creative – which is a very special skill indeed.

We had a good rapport, this Nuala man and me. We joked a lot, we laughed a lot, and he kept telling me he knew who my ancestors were and that because he knew my ancestors he had some sort of power over me. He didn't realise that I had already learned that my ancestor came from the sago tree – the traditional Nuaulu explanation of where white people come from. A few minutes before I took this picture I told him that I knew about the sago and I caught him looking at me in a way as if to say: 'Who are you? How did you know this?' It was a special moment.

One of my dearest friends, Lars Fält was a captain in the Swedish army. He began survival training in the Swedish Armed Forces and I was immensely privileged that he introduced me to the North.

This picture was taken while we were on a dog–sledding trip together. We stopped at a remote cabin and Lars was consulting the visitors' book when I took this photo. He has just found an entry made some twenty years earlier when he and his young wife Louise visited this cabin on skis.

Lars is a very special man, one of the old men of the northern frontier. You can't judge what somebody knows by their external appearance. Today people proclaim themselves experts far too quickly but you can only tell over time spent together on the trail.

This is a timeless mother and child composition – it could be repeated anywhere there are humans. The quality of the light and the warmth of the Mongolian people made it a very special moment. I have many fond memories of these wild and resilient people, who made us very welcome. For me the timelessness is intensified by the clothing and the colours reflecting the special Mongolian light. Timeless also is the warmth of human friendship that these people show to each other in such an empty landscape.

This is just one of the Mongolian men we worked with but I happen to like the photo; again it is somehow timeless. Yet in his face is the story of the weather he has lived through, both natural storms and political storms. His smile is that of a free independent Mongolian. Although time here seems to stand still, in fact it does not.

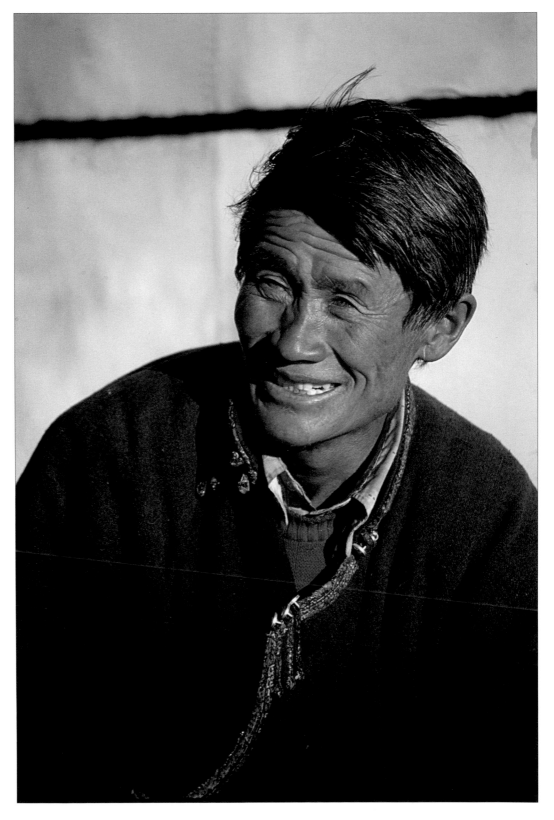

From all directions Mongolian people arrived to watch the horse race, wearing their finest clothing, such as these remarkable sunhats, and their *dels* (colourful jackets). When taking portraits of people, I try to use a wide-angle lens rather than a telephoto lens. This means you have to be close, and to be close means you have to develop a rapport. These gentlemen were happy to let me take their portrait, and that trust only comes from being close to the people and being prepared to rub shoulders with them and join in with their world.

This Evenk child is in a cradle that was used by her parents and grandparents when they were infants. For a nappy, either dried sphagnum moss or softly pounded and powdered dead wood is used. The child is encased in blankets behind a roll bar stitched to the outside to prevent accidents. When mosquitoes are in the air the whole cradle is covered with a mosquito net. At other times the cradle can swing from trees in the breeze. Here it is propped up against packs of goods brought by reindeer as the parents set up camp.

The child watches everything that is going on. I suspect that infancy in a cradle built like this encourages a very high degree of observational skill because the child can't reach out and touch anything. This method of raising young has been used in the boreal forest throughout the Northern Hemisphere.

This is Leo, a Shoshoni Indian in Wyoming. I like the quality of the light in this picture. Everything came together. He was very patient with me – I use an old-fashioned camera. He knew that he could trust me – we'd built a very strong working relationship. And he's a good man. He's one of those men who no matter what life throws at him, he'll constantly stand up whenever he's knocked down. People like him, just like the lodge pole in the background, are the supports of the community itself. In his hands are beautiful bags made from the feet skins of elk, which are very traditional.

Sam Cox is a sound-recordist I worked with on many of my early shoots. On the left we're in the Australian bush, in Arnhemland, and on the right we're in Labrador at –40ºC. On both occasions he was repairing vital bits of equipment. He's a sound-recordist who brings other skills with him, which is exactly what you need on these expeditions because things inevitably go wrong. Whenever there was a mechanical problem Sam would leap to the task – he's a man who enjoys the challenge of fixing things. I have very fond memories of working with him on many expeditions.

index

First published in Great Britain in 2008 by
Hodder & Stoughton
An Hachette Livre UK company

1

Edited by Gill Paul
Designed by Ned Hoste/2H

A CIP catalogue record for this title is available from the British Library

ISBN 978 0 340 96148 3
Printed and bound by Mohn Media in Germany.

Hodder & Stoughton policy is to use papers that are natural, renewable and recyclable products and made from wood grown in sustainable forests. The logging and manufacturing processes are expected to conform to the environmental regulations of the country of origin.

Hodder & Stoughton Ltd
338 Euston Road
London NW1 3BH

www.hodder.co.uk